View From The Hill

ANNELI SINKKO

Armour

View From The Hill

© Anneli Sinkko 2003–2004, 2025

Published by Armour Books
P. O. Box 492, Corinda QLD 4075 Australia

Images: karegg | Depositphotos, 'The beautiful beach of Yeppoon in the north of Australia'; Musti, by Anneli Sinkko;
newspaper: northseastudio | Creative Fabrica
cat icon: AnuchaSVG | Creative Fabrica

Interior Design and Typeset by Beckon Creative

ISBN: 978-1-925380-89-7

A catalogue record for this
book is available from the
National Library of Australia

All rights reserved. No part of this publication may be reproduced, stored in, or introduced into a retrieval system, or transmitted, in any form, or by any means (electronic, mechanical, photocopying, recording or otherwise) without the prior written permission of the publisher.

Note: Australian spelling and grammar conventions are used throughout this book.

View From The Hill

was originally published as a column in the Capricorn Coast *Mirror* weekly newspaper 2003–2004.

THIS COLLECTION OF heart-warming, folksy anecdotes published in a Yeppoon newspaper range across issues many readers share: ageing, walking for health, community, the support of pets.

Meet Anneli's cat, Musti, who possesses supernatural insights, mega-attitude and communication skills. His fur puffs up to receive fan mail—but could he even suffer depression? Nothing is as depressing as a depressed cat!

Then it gets interesting.

> He asked Anneli a profound question: 'Who is God?'
>
> I knew it! That day had arrived when I had to answer a very difficult question. 'Well, God is Spirit,' I answered, relying on my limited knowledge of the Bible.
>
> 'What is Spirit then?' asked Musti, looking me straight into eye.
>
> 'Well, you cannot actually see the Spirit,' I answered, 'but, you can feel him.'

'Explain this to me, taking into consideration that I have a very small brain,' said Musti.

Bravo to Anneli for braving deep existential issues in her columns! Which are now translated into book form. Having Finnish heritage myself, I know Finnish emigrants will relate to her observation that 'cleanliness is next to Godliness. But my dilemma is that, every time I am exposed to heat and humidity, I start sweating like Pavlov's dog, and possibly smelling like one too.' ☺

Ruth Bonetti
author of *Midnight Sun to Southern Cross*

The Bulleti

15th May 2006

Musti Bans Mothers Day

An unsuspected move today as Musti, the black and white cat of 18 Selvey Street declared that Mothers Day will be banned. This move is believed to be caused from the lack of sliced ham and cream that has not been

seved in recent months. A spoke person acting on behalf of Musti, a Mr P Winkle said that this action is warrented due to the changes in the Industrial Relations laws passed by the Government.

Contents

View From The Hill

View From My House

WE ALL LOVE our Capricorn Coast. We have the sea, the sand, and lovely people. Everybody is so friendly. It is like being part of a utopian community. When I look through my windows, I can see the waves and trees, and I feel very content.

But when I go down from my hill a different view presents itself.

Almost daily I see a young man who always walks barefooted along James Street and sometimes sits smoking near the entrance to Keppel Bay Plaza. This young man looks homeless, but he does not look unhappy. Perhaps a little bit lonely.

The girls who serve at checkouts at the supermarket greet me always so nicely, but they often look tired and I think: how good it is to be old. I no longer have to carry all the burdens of being young in today's world.

We should pay attention to the elderly who walk along so slowly and appear to be frustrated when people push and shove around them.

How about those people who buy only the three loaves of bread, that are on special, and nothing else? Or the young man, on his way to the caravan park, carrying so many shopping bags in the heat of the day that he could hardly walk?

These are the people who live in our neighbourhood. Stop sometimes, and say hello. In our community Christmas should never be over.

Yeppoon
29.12.03

Fat Cats

LET ME TELL YOU about my cat. He is a bad-tempered male, a Persian Cross, with a very finicky appetite and a mind of his own. He is also a miracle cat—a term he totally resents. You see, the last time I had to move before coming to Yeppoon, my cat took one look at my new rental residence and said: 'You must be kidding.' So he took off—for two months. But, after fervent prayers by my local Church, the elders of the neighbouring Sherwood Parish located him. The headlines in the local paper screamed: 'Prayers answered when Musti returns!'

When we moved to Yeppoon, the cat gave me a look: 'No more divine interventions.'

For the first few weeks he disappeared for several hours. I saw him walking smugly towards the local Sailing Club. He returned at night like clockwork covered with leaves and smelling disgustingly putrid! 'Just checking the local amenities,' he said. His eating habits also changed dramatically when another night my daughter's cat came to visit. One look at Perrie's 8-kilo form—and my cat decided it is time to put on some weight.

Until then I'd been the fat one in the family. Every time I put my diet plan into action, my daughter calls and says the disastrous words: 'Let's have some lunch together.' The fact is that there are just too many beautiful, delicious, tempting eateries in Keppel Bay. So, having moved to Yeppoon, both cat and myself are living in a culinary heaven.

Traffic Jam

I AM A VERY CAREFUL DRIVER. I have not had an accident since that fateful hot day, when I drove over a mattress south of Brisbane. They must be still talking about the day when I was waiting for a garage attendant to cut the mattress out in over 35° heat in the middle of peak-hour traffic while flocks of white stuffing were floating along a major highway. Well, at least I had the cleanest drive shaft south of Capricorn.

I love Yeppoon traffic! It is so serene—except during holidays, when you can see bewildered drivers going round and round and wondering whatever happened to the peaceful place we visited last year—off-season!

We love our visitors, but I have a thing about big cars. When I look up along a silvery side of a four-wheel drive from the depths of my own very small blue car, I am filled with very un-Christian feelings of envy, of which I hope to be forgiven. These feelings do not dissipate when our visitors go home, because many locals share this overwhelming fondness for the four-wheelers.

Traffic-wise, however, things will eventually get back to normal. Let us then be grateful for our sedate pace here at Yeppoon. This is the only place in the world, to my knowledge, where disabled car spaces are actually used only by disabled people. Good on you, Yeppoon motoring folk.

And remember, when schools start again, drive carefully around little children.

F2 Key

I LIKE COMPUTER GAMES. If I am totally honest, I am almost addicted! This is something I never admit to those well-meaning friends and relatives who question my fascination with computer games. I just tell them: it is good for me. Playing computer games keeps my mind active, my reflexes stay sharp—all of which is good for a person of my age.

In one particular game there is an option of the F2 key, which enables me to stop the game after I've stuffed up. And, I can resume the game in certain knowledge that I have an upper hand—however small.

In our everyday lives we also have a need for F2 key. You see, all of us, including myself, do occasionally stupid things. We lose our temper, and we cannot always blame the weather or the cat! Our own F2 key consists of three small words: 'I am sorry.'

It is a pity that these three words do not belong to my cat's vocabulary. Well he is, after all, just an animal. [He doesn't know that but, as he is asleep, he cannot make any comments.]

Like the F2 key in my computer game, to say, 'I am sorry' can give us a second chance. It gives us an upper hand. It may heal the past. These three words pave the way to peace, and that is what we all want here at Yeppoon and in our world in the coming year.

The Real Sauna

A FEW WEEKS AGO it was so hot and humid at Yeppoon that somebody said that this must remind you, Anneli, of the saunas you have in Finland. Well, not quite. First of all, we do not go to sauna fully clothed. So, in order to clarify this matter, let me tell you what it is like to go to sauna. And to make things really exciting: imagine a season of midwinter in Finland:

You enter the sauna naked, leaving all your dirty clothes outside. Your body is surrounded by hot steam, which increases every time more water is thrown on hot stones. Next you whack your whole body with birch-leaves. This removes all the old skin and dirt. Then you wash yourself. And then you rinse yourself clean. You feel like a newborn baby. But wait—there is more. After your body and soul feel totally pampered, soft, and so very, very clean—you go outside, still in the raw, and wash yourself with soft, freezing cold snow. This latest act of cleanliness braces your body and soul, hits you within with all the power and ritual of bathing to the extreme—and you will never be the same again.

Consequently, the childhood memories of sauna remain with me. I still think that that cleanliness is next to Godliness. But my dilemma is that, every time I am exposed to heat and humidity, I start sweating like Pavlov's dog, and possibly smelling like one too.

Mobile

I HAVE A MOBILE PHONE. It is something I keep just in case, and I usually pay my monthly bill, and forget about it. One day when I was going shopping I said to my son: 'Should I take my mobile with me?'

'Mum, it is called a "mobile" for a reason. It is called "mobile" because it moves wherever you move.'

Well, I took it with me. But I have to tell you: nobody ever rings me on my mobile. Why is that? Simple, I hardly ever give my mobile number to anybody.

And it is also most peculiar that I usually think in English, but when it comes to my mobile number, I only remember it in Finnish. Weird!

I've also noticed that there is a certain mobile etiquette. I always turn my mobile off when I go to Church, I am sure God has other ways of communicating with me—should He so wish. It is, however, entirely another matter when you go to a meeting. I leave my mobile on, for a simple reason that should anybody ring me, I would appear to be a very important person who has to keep in touch—even during a meeting.

Vanity of vanities!

Good people of Yeppoon, remember that you cannot use your mobile whenever you are driving a car. Expect extra heavy penalties should you be caught talking on one! Not that anybody I know ever uses her mobile when driving.

Leadlight—Communications

I'VE ALWAYS BEEN an admirer of leadlight windows. They give you a certain inner peace, and occupy children during boring sermons. I actually have a book on how to make leadlight articles. So, what have leadlights to do with communications?

The other night my son said to me: 'I've been looking at leadlights on the web.'

'Oh', I said, 'I have a book on leadlights.'

'Are you sure, Mum?' he said.

So, I showed him my book on leadlights.

'Oh Mum, you are so funny! *[I am?]* Not that kind of lights: it is spelled LED, which means *light emitting diode*.'

So, having somehow mastered the English language, I now have to face led-lights! I cannot keep with all these new words. LED-lights, indeed!

We have all these marvellous ways of communication: telephones, mobiles, emails, SMS, faxes and, if we are not at home—answering machines. I sometimes wonder what is happening. Doesn't anybody write letters anymore? As an older person, I sometimes feel it difficult to keep up with modern concepts, not to mention new technologies.

The communication between people, all kinds of people, is something that is so basic to all of us—in order to be heard we need to be understood.

Fortunately for me, my God also speaks Finnish.

Just Swimming Along

HAVING ORIGINATED in the Land of Thousands of Lakes, I love swimming. I was not too attracted to the waters of Keppel Bay after being told that one of the accessories I will need for my dip in the sea is vinegar. So, where can I then have a swim?

I found out there is a pool at Cooee Bay. So, one morning I took my togs and headed for the pool. It was quite warm and I was looking forward this refreshing treat. I entered to the complex, paid my dues, put my swimming costume on, and in I went.

That morning I shared the pool with some girls from St. Ursula's—it was lovely. There I was, like a big whale floating around surrounded by all these little minnows. I really enjoyed myself. Until there came a time when I decided to go home. How do I get out of here? You see, to my horror I realised that when I tried to swing my leg to the steps, I couldn't do it. Fortunately help was at hand: 'Try the other end, it is meant for little children, and it should be easier.'

Well, my dignity no longer intact, I managed to reach the steps at the shallow end. And my eternal gratitude goes to those girls from St. Ursula's without whom I would be still bathing in the cool waters of Cooee Bay swimming pool.

Musti for Mayor

My cat Musti follows local events carefully. When he found out that local Council elections were in the offing, he started to plan his election campaign. 'Musti for Mayor,' he cried.

One of the first things he promised was a large grant to the local pound. In addition he envisaged air-conditioned accommodation for the clients together with intensive counselling by trained animal psychologists. Being an avid reader of theological books, he wants to expand this section in the local library. He also intends to facilitate a cat-door to these popular facilities.

He is going to approach the electorate with plans of declaring Rosslyn Bay Harbour as a dog-free zone.

Further, he will increase the Council's social budget in order to organise nightly entertainment with belly dancers and live mice at the otherwise empty Keppel Bay Plaza.

In addition, all the boaties who regularly bring fresh fish to the Mayor's office will be able to fly the new

Mayoral Flag in their vessels, granting them unlimited access to secret locations known only by this candidate.

Seeing that the author of this column has been elected as Musti's campaign manager, unopposed, an approach was made to the present Mayor of our beautiful Livingstone Shire for comment.

Unfortunately, Mr Ludwig was on holidays.

Hump Days

WE ALL HAVE THEM—hump days, that is. So, what is a 'hump day'? For the staff at our beloved weekly, *Mirror*, it is Wednesday. This was a revelation to me, since this is the first time I had ever heard the term 'hump day'. I was let in on this secret celebration: it is the day when all the work is done and there is this certain satisfaction in the air that all is well in the Land of Livingstone Shire.

We all have them. High school students experience them on the week when schoolies start. If you have had a driving test and have passed it, that is truly a hump day; and your first payday is definitely a hump day. I have hump days usually on Sundays, whether I am preaching or not. On Sundays I am always grateful that I did not make any major blunders during the previous week and I am looking into the future and wondering what will happen next.

Honestly, think about it! You might have your own hump day and did not even realise it!

We here at Yeppoon have 'humps' everywhere! They surround us! So what are they? The hills, the hills!

Even the space net at the foreshore is sort of hump. Just look how do our children enjoy climbing it. We here at Yeppoon live in an elevated atmosphere; maybe we should have a Capricornian Hump Day to celebrate the small joys of life.

Volunteers

MY CAT COMES from a long line of felines who believe that humans were created to serve them. Therefore, I was totally amazed when Musti asked me if he could do some volunteer work at a Nursing Home. I smelled a rat! 'What would you do at a Nursing Home?' I asked.

'Oh,' he answered, grooming his whiskers, 'I heard that they serve excellent afternoon teas.'

Really, I should have known better. He was not thinking of the elderly people in need of comfort and company; no, he was thinking of his stomach!

So, I thought, it's time to educate Musti. I took out an Oxford Dictionary and read: 'A volunteer is a person who offers, undertakes, or performs a service on one's own initiative.'

'And,' I added, 'a volunteer does this service without any hint of monetary or culinary reward! They do it because they are interested in helping others and meeting likeminded people.'

'Really?' said the cat. 'Then it is a totally human thing; I am just an animal.'

So I explained what the volunteers do in our community. You can find them everywhere: in tuckshops, at the library, in the sea and on the beach. They give us service in art galleries, libraries, and community centres.

I told my cat that our community would not be such a loving, helping, and caring community without all those folk who offer their services just for the love of it.

'Hurray for our volunteers!' I said. But the cat didn't answer; he was asleep. Typical!

Ode to a Shopping Trolley

MY FIRST TRIP to Rockhampton was an occasion to remember. Having survived the journey from Yeppoon, and all those passing large cars, I arrived to my destination: the Shopping Fair. Because it was my first visit there, I was totally confused. After walking for ages, I said to myself, 'I am leaving. I am so tired.' But, horror of horrors, I couldn't find my car! So, I ascended the ramp once again and tried to get my bearings. I could hardly walk; I was so exhausted. Until I saw a lonely shopping trolley just waiting for me! I was saved. Leaning on the friendly arms of that blessed trolley, I finally got my bearings and found my way to my car.

I know that shopping trolleys do not have a good reputation. Their wheels seem to taking us wherever the trolley wants to go and sometimes they refuse to move at all. They are not loved by all and sundry. But—be grateful for them! And, I must say, here at Yeppoon we treat our shopping trolleys with respect, unlike in some southern cities. We do not use them for unworthy purposes. At Capricorn Coast you don't find shopping trolleys in gullies or in backyards. They stay where they belong—in orderly rows outside the shops.

However, their days may be numbered. I saw the other night a newcomer: all red and flashy, made of plastic. It looks like there is going to be shopping trolley war!

May the best trolley win!

View From The Hill

Party Animals

ON ELECTION NIGHT I was sitting at the veranda of the Mill Gallery, waiting for the opening of the art exhibition. Suddenly I saw a camel. Now, at that time I had no bubbly flowing through my veins, so I was not seeing things. After travelling in a trailer, the camel calmly turned down Mary Street, and then disappeared from my view. 'I just saw a camel,' I said.

'Oh, he just came from the Rydges Resort,' a friend of mine said.

'You must be kidding,' I replied.

'Oh no, they go there every week,' she said.

I have always associated camels with the wise men who came to see baby Jesus in Bethlehem. But now, a new horrible picture emerged in my mind: I saw camels sitting, every weekend, at Rydges' bar, drinking campari, and socialising with the guests. Further, I vaguely remember a certain polar bear having a cool one at the local. This explains why my cat used to go regularly towards the sailing club … the mind boggles! I need a reality check!

However, these mental images of alcoholic animals were soon dispelled, because Mr Richardson, the owner of the camels, told me that they work at the Rydges Resort. The strongest drink his camels, Coke and Sapphire, drink is 'coke'! Actually Coke the camel is quite famous far beyond our regions. Children love him.

So, next time you see a camel in the Central Business District of Yeppoon, rejoice. They are the hard-working ambassadors, the unsung heroes of our, ah-so-important, tourist industry. Hurray for the Camels of Capricorn Coast!

Timekeeper's Perch

IT IS A LONG TIME since I first came to Yeppoon and corrupted my daughter's cat with a purchase of shaved ham from the shops. The landscape of our town has changed, but not too much. The new buildings that have risen since I first came here have become familiar landmarks and we, as a community, have put up a good fight in order to keep Yeppoon's character.

But—there was a problem brewing. My cat, after his nightly excursion to the sailing club, told me that something odd is going on there. And, lo and behold, when I looked through my window one morning I saw scaffolding at the Keppel Bay Sailing Club.

Having survived the time when we fought against highrises, I became very suspicious. The council told me that our beloved landmark is having a facelift. The first rumour said that they are building a restaurant, then an observation tower. The plot thickens! So, I decided to ask the Sailing Club. And they told me straight from the horse's mouth: 'We are extending the timekeeper's office.' So, there you are, in order to time the races on our Bay, the timekeepers need to see them.

This is what is so good about living here. Nothing untoward can happen. People may talk, and wonder, but you can be certain that you always get a straight answer from the source—all you have to do is ask.

Pet Story

I JUST SAW IN THE NEWS that Spot, President Bush's dog, has died. Now this is not a major event, but I feel for him. As any animal lover knows, the passing of a pet is distressing, almost heartbreaking. A friend of mine, a minister down south and a total cat-lover, told me once that a family called him for a visit because their dog has died. And he did, what good ministers do: he gave a funeral for the dog—in their backyard. Now you may think that this is a bit over the top, but the family was able to grieve in a meaningful manner and receive comfort when they needed it.

Whether we have a dog, cat, or any other animal, we love our pets… After I've written this, my cat remarked: 'That's disgusting, I am not a pet. I am master of everything, a noble beast, who knows how to press your buttons.

'And,' he continued, 'if you look into a dictionary, the word "pet" is synonymous with "favourite, darling, choice, and preference". And that means that your cat or dog is your favourite companion, the darling of your days, he or she has chosen you and prefers to be with you of all the people on earth.

'Furthermore,' he said, 'every animal that finds a home with humans could tell a story of mystery, good luck, friendship, blessings, joy and lifelong food supply. Besides, it is a known fact that people with pets are happier, live longer, and are less lonely.'

That's my cat!

Tuckshops

THINGS HAVE CHANGED enormously since I was at Primary School. Every year we had to collect berries and mushrooms from the local woods just to complement the food offered at the school. And the lunches consisted mainly of pea soup.

I particularly remember one such occasion: there were hard black rocklike pieces in my pea soup. Later on, I found out that the hard work done by our school dentist had just gone to the bottom of my bowl!

But I will never forget those delicious moments when, at High School, we snuck out to the local bakery and stuffed ourselves with fresh jam doughnuts. The results of these escapades can still be seen on my hips.

When my own children went to school, things were not much better. I still remember peeling soggy tomato sandwiches from the bottom of their school bags.

But now, a new era has entered a local tuckshop. After a fruitful discussion with the Yeppoon High School Canteen, I was presented with a list of gourmet snacks: pies, sausage rolls, milk drinks, fruit drinks, salad boxes, a variety of sandwiches, fruit boxes, hot dogs, pizzas, lasagnes, and my favourite—chili-chicken burgers!

And—they also cater for special dietary requirements.

To top all this, they also offer ice creams and ice-cups in the afternoon. Well, as I am still in a state of having tomato-sandwiches for lunch, I wonder if, when the next lunch hour arrives, I could sneak into the High School for a snack.

I wonder if they welcome visitors with cats?

Attitudes

ON INTERNATIONAL WOMEN'S DAY I was standing on the veranda of the Keppel Sailing Club and watching seagulls. They went up and down, making the most of the movement of the air-currents. Then I saw something odd. One of the birds was floating in the air backwards! Maybe I was going mad and seeing things. However, as there was nothing stronger than lemon-lime-and-bitters in my glass, I must have seen the impossible. And no matter how hard I gazed, I never saw that seagull again. Maybe it flew to a place where gulls with attitude go. I'll never know.

But the vision of this gull flying backwards made me think: how to spot people with attitude. What then is an attitude? Well, according to my trusty old dictionary it is 'a habitual mode of thinking and feeling.' More than often we associate the word 'attitude' with bad behaviour.

A thought came to me. People with an attitude are, like my seagull, looking backwards. Quite often their attitude stems from what happened to them—in the past. And this past experience colours their present—

sometimes bad—behaviour. And, consequently, they cannot see what positive things could be before them in the future.

They fly, like my gull, pointing their bottoms towards tomorrow.

Beautiful Girls of Yeppoon...

DID YOU KNOW that March is Women's History Month? To celebrate this the Yeppoon Library presented a *Women's Stories—Histories of Livingstone* morning. Thus I've been knee-deep in the wonderful stories of the extraordinary women of our past.

When I listened to the stories one peculiar thing came to the fore. All women had 'M' in their name!

Mary Rattenbury [1878–1937] was a well-loved poet whose writings spoke so vividly of the events of her life experiences. She also wrote *Beautiful Girls of Yeppoon* and corresponded with Mr Doyle of *Sherlock Holmes* fame. She was truly a lady before her time when she envisaged votes for women!

Auntie Mabel from Darumbal Tribe, besides being a well-known artist, was also the first indigenous woman ever to enter politics. She was a Livingstone Shire councillor in the early 1970s. That was just a few years after the indigenous people received the right to vote!

Mary Atherton's life gave insight into the hardships of the early days. Matron Gertrude Everil 'Gus' Moore, recipient of the Order of the British Empire, was known at St. Brendan's College for her 'Moore-medicine'. And we should not forget Mary O'Brien, a local historian, who shared her research with other people in the know about these extraordinary women of our past.

So, there you are: Mary, Mabel, and Matron Moore—what is it with the letter M? Somebody enlighten me.

Well, I did name my cat Musti! And, our *Mirror* is still situated in Scandal Alley.

But that is another story.

What Is This Thing Called Love...?

MY CAT WAS READING the dictionary. All of a sudden he looked at me and said, 'What is this thing called *love*?'

'Well,' I said, 'there is *agape, eros...*'

'Don't go all Greek on me,' he interrupted. 'Use concepts I can understand.'

As my cat insisted that he can handle this—he is, after all, over eight years old—I began. 'When it is cold outside, or raining, and it is night, you come to my side and press your body against me, and I let you stay—that is love.'

'How come?' he asked.

'Well, we both give each other something that is pleasing to both of us. But,' I continued, 'when you sit outside the fridge because you know I have shaved ham there and do not move until you get it... that is lust. You are lusting after my last piece of ham, which you actually must get because you are extraordinarily fond of it!'

My cat looked at me scornfully, perhaps thinking about all the other treats in my fridge, which I did not give him. Then he said, 'What would I know about lust—you had me fixed!'

I was speechless!

I knew it. He is too clever by half, and I should have never got myself involved in this discussion. With this notion in mind, I opened the fridge, made myself a ham sandwich, and gave a little sliver to my cat.

Thus, I inadvertently crossed the fine line between love and lust.

On Becoming Old

MOST YOUNG PEOPLE, perhaps fortunately, think they never get old or sick. Getting old is something that does not concern them. They think that they will live forever. And that is the way it should be—how could the young ones otherwise be so full of hope and indestructible life force?

However, the old age does not creep upon us suddenly. We just tend to ignore the signs. We ignore the signs of old age until we find out that we need—horror of horrors—dentures!

We also may get physically hurt or sick. Then we find ourselves at the doctors and at the mercy of numerous pills or even worse— a surgeon's knife. We, the elderly, are asked to take it easy: 'You are not as young as you used to be!'

So, you may ask, if old age comes inevitably to all of us with its alarming disabilities, where do all those feisty old people come from? You see these grey-haired warriors at the beach walking with the best of us. They are the backbone of our churches and charitable organisations; they learn to use computers and some even go back to university! They even eat more fresh vegetables—as their mothers told them in the first place!

Well, the answer is simple. They, having reached the wisdom of old age, now show to the younger ones how the business of life should have been done in the first place.

By doing the right thing and by being motivated!

Water Deceptions

I DO NOT WATCH much television. The programs I like to see are on the ABC which, in my television at least, turns fuzzy at night. However, I do watch the local news and current affairs. The other night I saw a program where they tested the bottled water against the tap water. It appears that they are both just 'water'!

Well, I knew that! You see, when I was at the university in Brisbane, all the students could be seen walking around with bottles of designer water in their hands. It was an 'in' thing. Since I could not afford to buy this excessively expensive liquid, I decided to get just one of the designer bottles which I filled with tap water and walked around, with my beautiful water bottle, secretly enjoying my successful deception.

Water is also an important symbol in Christian tradition. However at the theological college, we young and irreverent candidates of religion had a joke about it. 'There are three grades of ministers. The first group washes with water. The second actually drinks it. But the elite, the third group—they walk on water.'

I, at least, fill the first two categories. [Yes, there is water in my occasional glass of Merlot!] But, if you consider that Finnish lakes freeze solid during the winter, I could say that I have actually walked on water! But that was then—now I just lumber around the beautiful shores of Keppel Bay and enjoy the view across our 'water'.

Top Cats

WHEN I OBSERVE my cat I realise that he has his favourite places. He particularly likes to sit on top of the meter-box, perhaps because of the view. Or, come to think of it—perhaps he just likes to be higher than anybody else.

But, when it rains or is too cold, my cat will come in like a rocket, curl in a dry spot [of course, after he has his snack!] or, luxury of luxuries, lie down in front of the heater. He knows how to be comfortable. In his own mind, he is the master of his universe, the top-cat of our household.

Through television I sometimes get a peek of the top-cats of our society and their habitats. Particularly in the 'renovation' shows, nothing seems to be too expensive or good for the recipients. They get new shining stoves, plasma screens… the list is endless. While watching these shows a thought enters my mind: why don't these shows portray everyday people—well, like me? I could do with a new stove… but, on the other hand, perhaps my place is beyond rescue.

But honestly, in today's world, there seems to be too much emphasis on the latest gadgets, too much emphasis on luxury. My cat has taught me a lesson. Unlike his owner, he wouldn't give a hoot for a new stove. All he needs is the basics: food and shelter—and, an occasional cuddle.

Loudest Miaow in Town

I AM, PERHAPS by accident of birth, quite a self-centred person. Some would say, mistakenly, that I have a huge ego. But that is not really so. Ask my cat, he can vouch that I am kind, loving... actually totally decent person—for a human. Having come to Yeppoon I have learnt to relax and let my apparent ego go under the waters of Keppel Bay. Good riddance!

We at Yeppoon are so easygoing that some 'newcomers' praising our relaxed atmosphere tell me that they wonder how could they ever have lived anywhere else. They, like me, have succumbed to the charms of Yeppoon, never to leave.

And I have learnt, that to be a true Yeppoonite, you have to be a special person. Folk with loud mouths or big egos do not survive here. Here at the Capricorn Coast, we not only know everybody else, but we almost know what others think—like my cat. He knows what I think before I do. He is also very vain. Grooming himself in front of the mirror [not our beloved *Mirror*], perhaps thinking of his sacred but distant cousins in Persia, he remarked, 'There should be a National Cats'

Day in Yeppoon. Rewards would be given to the most handsome cat in the district.'

He is, in all likelihood, already preparing his acceptance speech. How did he ever become a Keppel-side celebrity? How providential, therefore, that he does not speak to anybody else but me. Knowing him, better than anybody else, I would give him his reward, yes, for the loudest 'miaow' and largest ego in town.

Not Today, Love!

MY DOCTOR, BLESS HIM, told me that I should walk more. 'Walk on the beach,' he said. Now, I must confess that when I came to Yeppoon my health wasn't the best and the last thing in my mind was a walk on the beach. However, against my better judgment, I decided to take his advice. Thus one day, I parked my little blue car near the promenade and took some hesitant steps towards the steps leading to the beach.

Now I must tell you that I was not really looking forward to this. Even had I mentally prepared myself for this event, I did not feel comfortable. In my mind I could see myself sinking into the sand. I envisaged being stranded on the main beach and, instead of hearing the sound of the surf, I could almost hear the sucking sound my feet will make when I tried to pry them from the wet sand. And a thought crossed my mind: how could I get out of this walk without losing face?

Well, help came from an unexpected source. As I descended the steps towards beach I heard a bellowing voice, somewhere below me, calling: 'Hello, love!' I had stumbled into a hiding place of two visitors who were not only enjoying the sea views but also some liquid amber. With ungracious haste I turned around, left the beach, and said to myself: 'Not today, love!'

Henceforth I have stuck to the hills!

Obsessions

MY MOTHER USED to say, 'There is a place for everything and everything has its place.' This is simply called the routine of life. Without routine I could not survive. You know what I am talking about. In our household there is a cry to high heavens if my scissors have been moved. I have to know where they are—always.

Even my poor cat is a slave to routine. For some unknown reason every time he eats, he follows a rigorous routine of indicating his need for a snack. First he sits on the floor next to my chair and lifts his beautiful, pleading eyes to me. If I do not respond, which is usually the case, he touches my leg ever so gently with his well-sharpened claws. After this blatant display of raw claw-power I usually abandon whatever I was doing, stand up and walk him to his food bowl. Next I have to investigate that he actually has enough fresh and tasty nourishment—'fresh and tasty' being the operative words. Only then does he allow himself to graciously consume my meagre offerings of food.

But there is a downside to my obsession to routine. Not only do I have to know where everything is, but I also have to know where my children are, all the time, not to mention my cat. My children call my obsession 'she is just being mother', and my cat, well … he has no objection to routine, as long as it involves food.

Weird Customs

IN MY CHILDHOOD there was a special place for John the Baptist. His day was celebrated on June the 25th, just 6 months before Christmas. That day also happened to be the longest day in our year; in the northern part of Finland, the sun did not go down at all. Being weird people, we Finns combined the beheading of John the Baptist with much older tradition: the midsummer night fires. The fires were lit all along the thousands of lakes in my country. What comes particularly to mind is the bonfire of our next-door neighbours. This fire was unexpectedly enhanced by a hand-grenade, a relic of the winter wars. We kids found it in our lake. It was delicately hidden under the dry timber. It went up with a bang! But nobody got hurt.

The magic of old times did not stop at the fires. It was said that if a virgin went to the crossroads naked at midsummer night, she'd find her true love. Some would say that she would find more than true love, she would find trouble. Another custom, less daring, was to collect twelve different wildflowers and put them under your pillow. The man you see in your dreams will marry you that same year. I am not sure if it works, because I never tried it out.

I am sure we at Yeppoon also have weird and wonderful customs. Think about our pine-festival, regattas, and the early morning encounters in the pie-alley.

When Flowers Are Not Flowers

THE OTHER DAY I met an occupational therapist at Gracemere. She works with Blue Care and I was so impressed with her gift. She helps sick people to cope with their disabilities and helps them to discover their maximum potential. I said to her, 'I am sure you have received lots of flowers for your wonderful work.'

'Yes,' she said, 'and let me tell you of one of the most brilliant bouquets I received. I had this lady who could not walk well. And then, after receiving treatment for some time she told me that she had visited her next-door neighbour. I was so happy for her … you see, her neighbour lived in a high-set house, and my patient was able to walk up all those steps. I really was able to help her.'

How often we come across people who help others. And, amazingly, the greatest reward to them is to see that they have really helped somebody else. These quiet achievers do not need public accolades. Their rewards, their greatest and most brilliant bouquets of flowers, eventuate when they realise that they had really made a difference.

Look around you. I am sure that here at Yeppoon we have many of these everyday heroes. They serve us in art galleries, in op-shops, in Meals-on-Wheels, in various community organisations, in Blue Care, Lifeline, and the Red Cross. They serve us and receive, not flowers, but the satisfaction of work well done. Good on you all.

What's in a Name?

FOR SOME REASON today's society loves acronyms. So, what is an acronym? It is a short form of a name, like initials of the product or place. You know what I mean—think of a very Australian acronym: 'nimby'.

Now, Nimbin is of course a place in northern New South Wales where all sort of weird and wonderful Aquarians live. But to say that somebody is suffering from 'nimby-syndrome', we mean people who say that whatever is going to happen will definitely not happen in our neighbourhood. In other words: '**n**ot **i**n **m**y **b**ack **y**ard'!

An acronym I had problems with is SUV. 'What is an SUV?' I asked my son. And he explained that, in the 1970s in America, the government introduced new safety regulation for 4WD vehicles. So the manufacturers, in order to escape these new rules, no longer called their cars 'Four-Wheel-Drives' but 'Sport-Utility-Vehicles'. So, now you know. SUV is actually a Four-Wheel-Drive, which is masquerading as a Sports-Utility-Vehicle. The mind boggles!

Consequently, my dear reader, be careful with acronyms, they are a dangerous beast in disguise.

I'll tell you why. When I was at the Theological College, I used to add after my name the letters MIT. Now, when anybody asked me what it meant, I said calmly: 'Minister in Training'! That went down well as a joke, until somebody pointed out to me that MIT actually is an acronym of the Massachusetts Institute of Technology! You have been warned!

Powerless Dreams

I WAS WARNED BEFOREHAND. The electricity will be off; date and hours were given. But I forgot. So, there I was one Tuesday morning without power! The only phone that was working was my dreaded mobile, no computer, my washing was halfway through, and, horror of horrors, no cups of coffee … thank goodness it was not cold! Nothing moved in our household, except cat's tummy. He was asleep on my unmade bed. His body moved when he was breathing in and out and possibly dreaming of shaved ham.

All this brought my own unresolved dreams back to me. You see, at one time my late husband and myself dreamt of becoming totally self-sufficient. We planned of having solar power, toilet waste being recycled to get methane for cooking, a compost heap and a veggie garden, and enough land to have timber for our future fireplace.

Our dreams never came true, and I have a feeling that my cat is in a same awkward position. His dreams of shaved ham will not come true, not this time. You see, my fridge is still off, and so is the shaved ham I saved for my little furry friend.

Rockhampton Base Hospital

THE CAT USUALLY SLEEPS through the day. However, one fateful afternoon when I came back from Rockhampton, he was awake, gave me the look, and said accusingly: 'Where have you been?'

I explained to him that from June onwards I would be going to Rockhampton every day because I start working as a supply minister for Hospital and Blue Care Chaplaincy. 'You start working? That's a laugh,' said the cat. 'The way you like your comfort and food—you could be an honorary cat.'

I let that remark go and I told him about the Base Hospital, where I had been on that day. How ground floor handled emergencies, first floor—where the main entrance is—provides specialist services, pharmacy, café, and Pre-admission Clinic. There you can also find the Prayer Room if you need quiet time alone or see a Chaplain. I also told him how everything was marked near the elevators and, if you get lost, all you have to do is ask.

Musti took some time to take this in. Then he said, 'Isn't Rockhampton the place where they have the airport?

That terrible place where I was stuck on a rotating belt for hours before you picked me up. I was caged!'

'Maybe you need a trauma counsellor?' I said sarcastically.

'No, but a piece of shaved ham wouldn't go amiss,' said the cat, and fell promptly asleep.

Bonnet Protector

I HAVE BEEN TOLD that bonnet protectors are very practical when you drive along rough roads. Loose stones can damage your car but, with a protective shield on your bonnet, they just bounce away.

A thought came to me: where would I find an individual 'person-protector' who would shield me from all the unpleasant words and things that seemed to hit me sometimes left, right, and centre? You know what I mean.

If anybody were to invent such a thing it would become a very popular item indeed. I can just see the headlines: 'New invention, a personal protector, which is capable of protecting you from any of the unpleasantries of modern life.' And further, 'Guaranteed to protect against all nasty words, letters from the tax-office, demands for immediate payment etc. They will just bounce away, try it today!'

But seriously, how can we protect ourselves in these uncertain times?

Well, as far as I am concerned, I pray. So, what is prayer? First of all it is a dialogue. And, as in any interchange, there is a time when you speak and time when you listen. Dietrich Bonhoeffer, a Lutheran pastor who was killed during the Nazi years, wrote: 'Men go to God when they are sorely placed.' Whether you go to God or not, that is your personal choice. But it is good to know that you can, should you be 'sorely placed'.

But you also could say 'hello' to Him anytime—and see what happens.

Stating the Obvious

THE OTHER DAY I was driving along Anzac Parade. When I came to the pedestrian crossing, I automatically slowed down—like the good citizen I am. But then I had to stop altogether because there was somebody crossing the road. Two seagulls calmly took advantage of the pedestrian crossing which, by quite a fortunate accident, led to a fish and chips shop! By now you know an answer to the question: 'How do seagulls get to the fish and chips shop? They use the pedestrian crossing!'

Consequently, another 'stating the obvious' joke was added to my vast collection of 'elephant jokes'. So, what are the elephant jokes? Well, they used to float around when I was much younger, and slimmer. For instance, 'How do elephants get to the third floor? They go into the lift and press the button number 3.' Or, 'How can you fit four elephants in to a Volkswagen? You seat two at the back and two at the front.'

Elephants aside, the other night I went to my bathroom—not to count any elephants, mind you. Now, in there is a window near the ceiling, which is used generally by Musti the cat during his nightly excursions. And you never guess who was there. Not the cat, but a spotted cuscus! We looked at each other, both equally amazed. And it came to me: 'What is a cuscus doing in my bathroom? Well, it was having a bath, of course!'

Oh, the joy of the absurd!

Human Touch

THE OTHER DAY when I returned from my Chaplaincy work at Rockhampton, there was no sign of Musti the cat. I thought to myself: 'Well, he has just gone outside or maybe he is hiding under the roof—his favourite hideyhole.' But the day wore on and it was getting late. No sign of my cat! I was getting worried. I started to think of the consequences, if he did not return. I started to panic. In my mind I saw my next article for this *View from the Hill* column: 'Obituary for Musti'.

It was getting dark and I decided to call for re-enforcements. So I rang my son. Just as I started to talk to him, guess who walked in? Yes, it was Musti, smiling smugly at me: 'Now you know what it is like to be left alone for the entire day!'

I did not know whether to be angry or pleased, so I gave him his dinner and decided to let the matter drop.

All this, however, led me to think how not only animals but also we humans crave company and comfort that comes to us by loving contact. This is very evident when I walk along the corridors of the hospitals. So many people want to stop me for a chat and words of encouragement and comfort. Hospitals can be very lonely places. So, my friends, next time you know of somebody who is at a hospital, please give him or her a call. I know from personal experience that it will be greatly appreciated.

Fame

TODAY, BEING MY MORNING OFF, I visited *Mirror's* office. And there it was: Musti's first fan mail. A kind reader from Emu Park had sent Musti, and myself, a book called *The Cat's Out of the Bag*. I took it home, and now my cat cannot contain himself. 'This is perrrfect,' he said. 'I am famous.' He could hardly contain himself. His magnificent fur was all puffed up, and his whiskers stood up. He was so pleased with himself that he could hardly stay within his fur!

'Just a minute,' I said. 'I am the one writing about you.'

'But,' said his highness, Musti the Magnificent, 'every time I try to use the computer, you lift me down, and I can never finish my thoughts. You are just my ghost-writer!'

Really! At this stage he turned his back to me, a true sign of displeasure. 'What would you know?' he murmured through his ever-so-sharp teeth. 'You do not understand me.'

So, in order to make him feel better, I told him about all the famous cats of the past, how some have been detectives, while other have been worshipped as divine beings. Musti gave me the look and said: 'So it is really true what I heard the other day. Dogs have masters, but cats have slaves.'

And now I keep wondering, who let that 'cat out of the bag'.

What's in a Name?

I ALWAYS HAD SERIOUS DOUBTS about Musti's heritage. Even my vet, when he saw him as a small kitten, declared: 'Persian Cross!' And I thought that there is nothing Persian about my cat. He does not have the snub nose or the smug look of a Persian. He has remained without kith and kin until my daughter, bless her, found a Musti-lookalike on the web: 'Norwegian Forest Cat'. Now, this sounds much nobler than a 'Persian Cross', don't you think?

So, what is a 'Norwegian Forest Cat'? Well, they come in variety of colours, and in truth, some of them look exactly like my cat. Another notable similarity is that apparently those Norwegian cats are outdoor cats and sometimes behave like dogs.

Now, my cat loves outdoors. Nothing pleases him more than climbing to a highest point of the landscape. And there is more—he comes home when I whistle. Besides, he has this outdoor fur like his Northern cousins which, unfortunately, requires a lot of brushing, and sheds during summer.

However, this is the stuff dreams are made off. Maybe his ancestors once hunted with Thor, the main deity in Norwegian mythology. But does it really matter? He is my constant companion who at the moment is sleeping the sleep of the just under the television set. He does not know, nor care, what he is and where he came from. The only thing that matters to my cat is that he has food, shelter, love and an occasional sliver of shaved ham.

These are the things that make him happy—Norwegian or not!

Cat of Seven Lives

BECAUSE I'VE BEEN WORKING, Musti has not been a happy cat. Being a spoiled animal and a master of everything he expects me to be at his beck and call—all the time. But, this week brought home to me how much I also appreciate my furry friend.

Musti disappeared for 24 hours. I was so worried. However, just after I had informed all the concerned friends and relatives, and the local Animal Shelter [Barbo], the cat himself appeared from his secret hideout under the eaves. And he was not well.

So, next morning I took my treasure to his very own vet. And guess what? They figured out that he has had a traumatic encounter with a car. No broken bones, but missing claws!

Apparently some of his nails are, at this moment, stuck in a wheel of that unfortunate motor vehicle which came too close for comfort. No wonder Musti was so sick. He had suffered a major trauma!

After receiving painkillers, TLC, and antibiotics he was released to the loving arms of his family. Now he walks very carefully, sleeps a lot, and is manhandled twice a day in order to give him his antibiotics.

This is not the first time he has been on death's door. Last year he ate some poison and his liver almost gave up. If a cat has nine lives, as the saying goes, then Musti has already used two of them. I just hope that he will keep the remaining seven till a ripe old age!

Depression

DEPRESSION HAS BEEN a buzz-topic for some time. All of a sudden the powers-that-be have realised that many of us humans experience depression. In its simplest form depression can be called 'sadness over a loss'. What then are the signs? Well, you want to hide in a dark room and you sleep a lot, cry without any reason, and eat—comfort food!

Would you believe that my cat, Musti the magnificent, is depressed? Now, you may say, how is it that cats can experience depression? Well, it is a well-known fact that animals suffer from 'separation anxiety'; so, why not depression?

After his encounter with a speeding tyre, Musti has been definitely depressed. First of all he hid under the eaves and stayed there. He only came inside to eat. Now he has finally resigned himself to stay inside, and what does he do? He sleeps in his favourite chair, and only gets up to eat. He does not want to socialise. He occasionally grooms himself, just to keep some feline dignity, but otherwise he just has this look: 'Leave me alone, I am suffering.' He actually is depressed because he lost some of his claws which, as my vet tells me, will grow back.

Just looking at my cat made me depressed. I have lost my brave-hearted warrior cat!

He has made me feel guilty beyond measure.

And, dear reader, nothing is as depressing as a depressed cat!

Re-enactment

WHEN I WAS STUDYING counselling I did my internship at a clinic near the Gold Coast. This clinic specialised in Gestalt Therapy. Now, you may well ask, what is Gestalt Therapy? Well, it is a form of therapy where you confront your past fears by acting them out in a safe and controlled environment. This happens either by dialogue or play.

And that is exactly what my cat has been doing! He is much better, thank you very much, and part of his recovery is due to the fact that he is using the previously mentioned therapy. Now you, my dear reader, may think that I have rocks in my head. But, let me tell you what Musti is doing.

He goes to the nearby driveway and rolls over. Not just once, but several times. Then he looks at me and tells me, 'This is how it happened.' And yes, he is speaking to me again. He is re-enacting the dramatic rollover he experienced recently. The passing car must have given him a real rollercoaster drive! And yes, his paws are healing, and he is returning to the cat he was.

Of course my son, being wise beyond his years, tells me that Musti just likes to roll in sand. Be that as may be, I saw the other night how my cat was devouring books in my library. And, he just happened to be near the section where my counselling books are.

What next, Gestalt Therapy for cats?!

'Who is God?' asked the Cat!

HAVING SURVIVED his recent trauma my cat has become very talkative again. The other day he asked me a profound question: 'Who is God?'

I knew it! That day had arrived when I had to answer a very difficult question. 'Well, God is Spirit,' I answered, relying on my limited knowledge of the Bible.

'What is Spirit then?' asked Musti, looking me straight into eye.

'Well, you cannot actually see the Spirit,' I answered, 'but, you can feel him.'

'Explain this to me, taking into consideration that I have a very small brain,' said Musti.

'Well, you like sitting in the sun, don't you? You cannot see the rays of sun, but you can feel them.'

Then, for reasons known only to himself, he said: 'How come you worship Him, if you cannot see Him and only know about Him from a book?'

Really, my cat is getting too smart for his own good! And then a thought came to me and I said: 'Tell me what goes through your mind when you sit outside the fridge? Why are you doing it?'

'I am not worshipping the fridge, if that is what you are implying,' said Musti scornfully. And he continued: 'You know very well that I am after that last piece of shaved ham inside the fridge.'

'But can you see it?' I asked.

'No, but I know it is there,' replied Musti.

'Well, there you are. That is why I worship God. I cannot see Him but I know He is there.' Problem solved… I think.

Keeping Clean

MY SYMPATHY GOES to all of you Yeppoonites who work. During my time as a Blue Care Hospital Chaplain, my house started to look like a disaster zone. The disintegration started when my cleaning lady, bless her, decided to take a holiday. During my time of employment my dishes multiplied like loaves and fishes, I had a cranky cat, dirty windows, a neglected garden, and a house that looked like a bombsite. Now, being again classed among the happy retirees, I have to do some serious cleaning in my place.

What is it with cleaning? Where does all the dirt come from? Why don't things stay in their allotted places? They seem to have a mind of their own and eventually you can't find anything. Or is there some secret place that exists only to spew dirt on my house?

I looked at the cat for answers. 'Don't look at me,' he said. 'I am just a cat.'

'Thanks a lot,' I replied.

'Besides,' said the cat, 'you are going wrong way about it.'

'How come?' I said. 'What would you know about cleaning?'

'But I do,' Musti replied, 'I am doing it all the time. How do you think I stay so beautifully groomed? It is hard work and I am at it—continuously.'

Consequently I have learnt that in order to keep the house clean, I also have to be at it all the time. Well, it used to be that wisdom came out of the mouth of babes—but out of the maw of Musti, really!

Reality Bites

MANY OF THE GOOD FOLK at Yeppoon have asked me a question: 'Is Musti a real cat?' Even the people at my local Uniting Church have wondered whether he is just a figment of my imagination. Consequently, the first thing those selected few who have visited my abode ask is: 'Where is the cat'? And having feasted their eyes upon his magnificent form they declare: 'It is him, he is truly a real cat—fancy that.'

Now the other night, when Musti was watching television, he saw a commercial of an upcoming movie on Garfield. 'What is this?' he said. 'Who is this cat? Is he real? I've never seen a cat with orange fur before.'

'His name is Garfield,' I said, 'and he is not real. He is cartoon character created in 1978 by Jim Davis who grew up on a small farm in Indiana.'

'And', I continued, 'Garfield is nothing like you. He is fat, lazy, and loves lasagna.'

Musti was, quite uncharacteristically, quiet for a while. Then he said, 'What is lasagna? I have never tasted lasagna! I have never been offered lasagna. I will go to my grave without a taste of lasagna. You have deprived me of this exquisite delight.'

As usual, I was speechless. And then it came to me: 'Only cartoon cats with orange fur eat lasagna. Real cats, like you, eat shaved ham—trust me.'

Consequently, he stepped in front of the fridge, and gave me the look: 'How about a slice of real cat food for a real cat?'

What's in a Name?

I'VE BEEN ALWAYS fascinated by etymology. What is etymology, you may ask? Well, it is the science that looks into the origin and history of words. Just to get you in the swing of things here is an example: The word 'kassa' in ancient Greek meant a 'table'. In Russian the same word is used for a 'bank'—reflecting the ancient use of a moneylender's table. In Finnish this same word is used for a 'teller machine'—and in English our word 'cash' and it's derivative 'cashier' originate from the same Greek word 'kassa'.

And, just in case you wonder where does Musti's name come from? Musti in Finnish means 'blackish'—and is actually a dog's name. But since Musti behaves like a dog, and does not know that he is not a dog, we do not have any problems—yet.

When I walk along Yeppoon Streets, I wonder where all these names came from. Who is James? I know that some of the bridges in our area have been named after local identities, but Queen Street; which queen are be talking about—surely not the queen of the Pineapple Festival? And somebody tell me, please, who is John?

Is it John the Baptist, John the evangelist or some other unknown John from our shadowy past? Please inform me.

And where is Bill's place—yet to come? The mind boggles!

Cats Don't Cry

MUSTI WAS INSPECTING various cardboard boxes in our living room. 'What are you doing?' he asked.

'I am packing books,' I said.

'May I ask why?' said the cat.

'I have been asked to be a minister at Rockhampton South. I am moving,' I replied.

'Well, I am not moving anywhere,' said the cat. 'I don't like moving.' And he let his eyes glide towards Keppel Bay and, inadvertently, also towards the little birds that inhabit my bottle brush. 'I like it here. Why would anybody want to move away from Yeppoon? What's the matter with you? I thought you were happy here.'

Musti and I have had this conversation before. How can I explain to him, again, that to work for God is more important to me than anything else? How can I tell Musti that there are matters that go beyond our worldly expectations? How could I explain that I cannot but go? So, I don't even try. But—and this is for all my human friends, in the near future you will find me at the Campbell Street Uniting Church. As for Musti, he will live at Yeppoon till his ripe old age in the care of my son.

So, dear readers, it is goodbye not only to my cat, but to all of you. And I would like to thank you all for your support and comments, which you have given me on many happy occasions. I will miss you all, as I will miss my family, and Musti. Fortunately cats don't cry—even though humans do.

Thank you all.

Anneli Sinkko

ANZAC Day 2004

I JUST HAVE READ letters from the war—both from France and Gallipoli. Those memories of these terrible times are distant for me but I know that, when my mother was very young, the whole of Europe was in turmoil. The events at Gallipoli and France happened at the same time that my own country, Finland, fought for independence.

But I have also my own memories of a war. One of the earliest recollections from my childhood is when I was looking out through our kitchen window. I saw bombs shattering our lake. I could hear the planes—the enemy planes—flying overhead. After that event we devised a cellar, into which we escaped every time the alarm sounded. I was scared. During the Winter War we had to move into the safety of our countryside. Many children were evacuated to Sweden. My father served in the army.

During ANZAC Day we are asked to remember. We all have our own personal memories of times of war and conflict. And while we remember with gratitude and even fondness those who fought in the wars, let us also do our utmost so that our children never have to be scared.

This Day, the ANZAC Day—let all of us pray for peace.

www.ingramcontent.com/pod-product-compliance
Lightning Source LLC
Chambersburg PA
CBHW051712180726
48283CB00004B/1310